Furniture Refinishing
Made Easy
by
Dave Sands

LONE
PINE

Homeworld

The Publisher:

Lone Pine Publishing
#202A, 1110 Seymoour St.
Vancouver, B.C.
V6B 3N3

Lone Pine Publishing
#206, 10426-81 Avenue
Edmonton, Alberta
T6E 1X5

Canadian Cataloguing in Publication Data
Sands, Dave
        Furniture refinishing made easy
(Homeworld)

Includes index.
ISBN 1-55105-022-6

1. Furniture finishing. 2. Wood finishing. I.Title. II.Series.

TT199.4.S26 1992 684.1'043 C92-091752-6

Original Compilation: *Keith Ashwell*
Editorial: *Lloyd Dick, Debby Shoctor, Gary Whyte*
Homeworld Editor: *Lloyd Dick*
Cover Illustration: *Linda Dunn*
Original illustrations: *Doris Chaput*
Printing: *Friesen Printers. Altona, Manitoba, Canada.*

The publisher gratefully acknowledges the assistance of
the Federal Department of Communications, Alberta
Culture and Multiculturalism and financial support
provided by the Alberta Foundation for the Arts in the
production of this book.

Contents

Furniture Refinishing

This book is for anyone who must repair or refinish a piece of furniture and who wants to do it in the most efficient way. It will stress simple and straightforward methods using readily available products and techniques that produce good results. It's also aimed at anyone with imagination who is prepared to try to transform a tacky-looking but solid chair, dresser, chest or table into a piece of furniture that could probably match anything recently made in terms of style and durability.

What this book is not about is antique restoration: if you own a genuine antique, treat it like an investment. Anything you might do to it may reduce its value, so it's worthwhile to spend money on professional work, if that expense will enhance your investment. If not, leave it alone, and let the person who may one day pay you a lot of money for your antique do the spending. However, most old furniture is not antique, merely old.

Old furniture has one great difference from new — its material. Old furniture is likely to be made out of real wood, and therefore worthwhile repairing and refinishing, both for its value and its usefulness to you, not to mention that

A Note

At the end of this book, under **Terms and Words,** you will find much detailed information. Please check this section for words used in the portion of text referring to your next stage of refinishing before you begin that stage. You might even find it interesting to scan this section before starting your project.

Also, after some sections you'll find blank pages for your own notes, regarding what materials you've used, and on which pieces of furniture. When filled in as you work, these pages become your reference for later projects and also for touch-ups in the years to come.

Always remember your own personal safety when refinishing furniture.

buying new furniture of the same quality of materials and construction may be impossible for many reasons, price being one.

Refinishing your furniture may be something you've wanted to do for a long time. Perhaps someone has left you with something you've stored out of sight because it's painted fire-engine red or a livid green. It could be a nice little coffee table that's been painted black, orange or some outrageous colour, or a spindle-back chair that was obviously pretty long ago. You may even have picked up a good, but badly finished piece for nothing at a garage sale or an auction.

Refinishing is your choice when you're dissatisfied with what you've got or curious about what might be under all those layers of paint, time and other people's taste. It's also a great way to have good-looking furniture that you can take pride in without having to spend a fortune.

Preparation for Refinishing

When planning to strip and re-finish furniture, keep in mind that you'll be using chemicals strong enough to dissolve paint and "burn" wood. You'll be using sharp tools, finishes composed of strong chemicals with powerful effects, and you will be working in the presence of a lot of fine dust, strong smells and under some stress created by the fact that you want to do good work and may be new at the job.

First things first means safety first. Wear old, clean clothes — long sleeved shirts, full length pants, thick socks and a good, old, closed pair of shoes. Do not wear sandals, cut offs, and T-shirts; they leave too much skin bare to splash, nick, soak and scrape. Wear work gloves and have kitchen style rubber gloves on when you're using paint removers. Your eyes deserve a pair of safety glasses that cover them from forehead to cheeks. Keep these glasses clean and unmarked by returning them to their box between jobs. Your head should have a cap, scarf or toque. And when you're generating any kind of dust — whether through sanding, scraping or sawing — wear a disposable face mask and save yourself a lot of hacking and coughing, which is nature's way of trying to get foreign material out of your lungs.

All of this may sound like too much trouble: but it's nothing compared to the trouble an injury could cause.

Work environment

A source of clean water is also important. Paint removers and thinners are caustic, so drops splattered on unprotected skin will burn if not promptly rinsed off. When working indoors, you need a space with a combination of adequate room, good ventilation, good light, cleanliness and comfort. Working outside provides good ventilation, but creates real problems with cleanliness; all but refinishing jobs can be done outdoors, with some precautions. If there are children or pets around, it's easy to forget that some hazardous materials may be left unprotected while you run to the store for some forgotten item.

Supplies

Any furniture refinishing project requires tools, supplies, power equipment, etc. These should be on hand before beginning the project, so make sure everything you use is stored properly.

Metal or glass bowls, or old paint cans

It is very important that empty paint or other cans be completely free of any adulterating materials or colourings. Have a good number of cans handy; one for each chair leg when stripping finishes, for example.

> ## *Warning!*
> Plastic is likely to dissolve when you pour in strippers; use plastic containers only for non-chemical uses, like parts, tools and storage.

Water

As already mentioned, many of the products you'll be using are chemically powerful, and it's important that any splashes onto exposed skin be rinsed off immediately.

Sponges, towelling, paint cloths

Rags should be clean, lint-free and soft. Old diapers are often recommended, because they are lint-free, don't scratch, and are a good size when held in your hand, but any similar quality of cloth will obviously do. These rags are required to mop up paint, glue or stripper splashes; to wipe off paint brushes; to apply and even out newly-applied stain; to buff polishes, clean off dust, and wipe your forehead. Keep an adequate number handy. More are always better than less, and they should not be mixed. Use them once and toss into a bucket of water if they've contacted oils, varnishes, solvents or thinners. This prevents refinishing disasters and the danger of fire from spontaneous combustion.

A tack rag

Buy them or make your own with turpentine and varnish drops on a cloth which is then wrung out tightly and kept sealed away from dust until it is needed, when it is invaluable in achieving dust-free surfaces. Use a tack rag immediately before applying any finish coat to any furniture, especially if has been sanded.

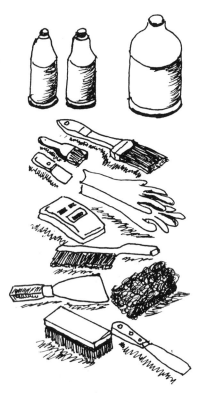

Bleach

Bleach is used to lighten bare or sanded wood, or to take out any stains in wood. Commercial or household bleaches differ in their strengths but both are still bleaches. Pure vinegar will effectively stop chemical actions that can eventually lead to "scorching" or unsightly blackening of certain portions of the woodwork.

Sandpaper

Sandpaper comes in many materials and grades. The types of abrasives available include flint, emery, garnet, aluminum oxide and silicon carbide. It comes in grades ranging from super fine to extra coarse. Always start out with a coarser grade and work your way to a finer one.

Steel wool

This is readily available at paint or hardware stores and for the beginning refinisher is easier to use than fine sandpaper. But for smoothing out mechanical cuts to the wood, sandpaper still remains the best method. Steel wool is sold in grades: the finest is usually graded 0000, but markings may vary.

Play it safe, work in safety

It is important to remember that any time tools (especially power tools), paints, chemicals and sprays are being used that others should be warned to keep a safe distance from the work area. If it must be left for any length of time, others must be instructed not to touch *anything*.

The same is true for family pets. A can of paint stripper accidentally knocked over can do great damage instantly.

Reminder: some of these stripping and thinning concoctions look like water if they're kept in a glass bottle or jar. Drinking them can be fatal to the unwary. There are so many opportunities for accidents that protection must begin early, and continue for the duration of the entire project.

Shellac or lacquer sticks

As these don't deteriorate with time, a reasonable selection of colours is always a useful investment, if only for repairing much-used furniture that has been scratched or otherwise damaged, and does not need a complete refinishing job.

Glue

Glue for furniture or general wood repair uses will be labelled as such. **"White"** glue will dry transparent, is inexpensive, easy to use and available everywhere under various brand names. **"Yellow"** glues are less often available but are stronger than white. **"Epoxy"** glues, which must be mixed just before use from their two components, resin and hardener, are the strongest, but most inconvenient to use. To be effective, glues must "cure" under pressure, either from weights or clamps.

Newspapers, tarps, or drop cloths

Wherever you work there will inevitably be a mess. A few layers of newspaper laid under the piece of furniture and covering approximately two to four times its size will avoid much clean-up time later. Cover the newspaper with a clear plastic "drop cloth" when you're stripping or finishing.

Brushes

Using any old paint brush simply won't work. Even an apparently well-cleaned brush may have paint pigments lurking near the handle area which can become loosened by a stripper and suddenly produce unpleasant stains. When refinishing furniture, use a brush for only one purpose or one finish, clean it carefully and allow it to dry. Good brushes cost money — but this is one area of refinishing where you should not economize. Varnishing or applying clear finishes requires good, expensive brushes. However, if you're staining, or brushing on strippers or paint removers, cheap or old brushes should be used.

Neutralizers and thinners

Water has already been mentioned, but it is also important to have on hand a large jug of plain white vinegar, a supply of mineral spirits, some turpentine, as well as thinners for all the paints or stains and finishes used (for diluting, as well as to clean brushes). Buy the thinners or cleaners recommended by the maker of the finish you're using. Most finishes are sold in complete lines—fillers, undercoats, thinners, finishes, etc.—and buying the same brand eliminates uncertainty and surprises.

Workplace

Refinishing is a necessarily messy business. Necessarily because you must apply a liquid to a solid surface, let it soften that surface and then remove both. Messy because none of this stuff is very attractive to have around. In addition, sanding and refinishing both create their own messes.

Checklist

* Establish a place where the job can be done and protect it (with newspapers, etc.); and seal it off, either by closing the door or hanging sheets of thin plastic from the ceilings and walls around the area.

* Choose a spot that's warm, well lighted, and dust free. Ideally, this is a room that's suitable for living quarters — a spare bedroom, etc.

* The ideal room isn't always available however, so compromise in terms of the job you're doing: stripping and sanding can be outside, basement, balcony, garage or carport jobs; gluing and clamping should be done in a warm, separate area because glue needs warmth (usually above 70°F) to flow and set, and the work, once clamped, shouldn't be disturbed.

* Perhaps a bedroom or family room area, with the floor covered while you're working and the job suitably draped to conceal it while it sets. Refinishing, especially with clear finishes, definitely has to have the cleanest, driest, least drafty place possible. Again, inside the house or apartment.

Work platform

Get whatever you're doing off the floor. You will do better, faster work with the job you're working on horizontal, no less than waist high, in good light. This means a work platform that is low, about 60 cm at the most, sturdy, and large enough to safely support whatever you're refinishing. Obviously, a platform for a dresser will be larger than one for chairs. If you can't walk all the way around your piece, or you want the convenience, build a "lazy susan" style rotating top on the platform. Turntable hardware is commonly available and inexpensive, and the time and effort saved is remarkable.

Any work platform should have a soft covering like old carpet, to prevent scratching or marking the new finish.

Personal Notes

Thinking about furniture

The world is so full of "genuine antiques" these days that it is impossible for them all to have come out of the workshops of the Chippendales, Sheratons, Heppelwhites or any of those old world master craftsmen. There are carpenters and factories today that specialize in making reproductions — some of which are sold as genuine — and in terms of an antique look and feel, it is possible to buy some very fine work indeed.

Other furniture may not have the credentials of antiquity but still has style and personal appeal, an appeal that could be over-looked at an "antique" sale. Or it may be a hand-me-down that has suffered from use and abuse, and from changes of taste and fortune.

Whatever it is, and however it was acquired, for some reason it interests you or you like it, or even more to the point, you need it because it's useful, but it's ugly.

Typical pieces

Chairs

Chairs are made in two ways: a platform and a frame style. Platform chairs (the familiar "captain's chair" is an example) have a solid seat or base, to which the legs, arms and back are attached, usually by round tenons set into round mortises. Frame chairs ("dining room" chairs) have a back made of single pieces that form the support for the back of the chair and the back legs. Side rails and front rails support the seat, and the front legs are separate pieces. They are usually jointed with dowels or with flat mortises and tenons, and the seat is separate and held on with screws and glue blocks.

Casework

Casework is a very general term applied to furniture with a box-like basic construction. Anything with doors, shelves, drawers or all three (like a desk) is casework. Joints in casework will usually be a combination of dovetails in the drawers, mortises and tenons in the frame, and rabbets or dados holding shelves, panels or glass. All three kinds of joints can work themselves loose. Screws are more common in casework than chairs.

Tables

Tables are usually made up of frames, with the top attached to apron pieces, and the legs attached to the apron. Screws, bolts and metal clips are common in tables, as are mortise and tenon joints, especially in pedestal tables.

Repairs

Whether found at an antique auction or garage sale, up in an attic, or in a son's or daughter's recently vacated room, you must first subject your chosen piece of furniture to an intensive examination.

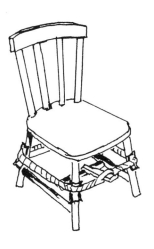

With all types of wood furniture construction, problems will arise in the joints, as a result of use and age. Low humidity — dryness — is a major threat to all furniture. If your furniture gets loose and squeaky only during the winter months, it's most likely a humidity problem, not wear. If joints are loose and weak year round, fix them as soon as possible: weakness in one joint intensifies the stress on others, and total collapse becomes more likely.

If repairs are necessary — for example, a leg is broken or a spindle loose, back panelling severely split, hinges loose or drawer pulls missing — the question is, can they be fixed? You'll find out that most can be, however, some damage requires skill and tools. The next question is, is it worth having an expert do the basic repairs before beginning this refinishing project?

Burlwood

Beautifully-figured walnut, usually known as burl walnut, is much prized as a veneer. This was the basis of a style of furniture produced by the great 18th century French cabinet-maker, Andre Charles Boulle. Burls are characterized by a grain pattern that goes everywhere and has no single direction. Other veneers will show a grain direction.

Even veneers that either have missing sections, or have lifted, can be easily repaired by a craftsman with patience. Veneers of all kinds of woods are often carried by woodworking supply shops, especially those specializing in restoration (listed in the Yellow Pages).

Cleaning

Having decided to restore this piece of furniture, it may dramatically improve after a good scrubbing with hot soapy water. But never use water on a veneered piece: it can ruin it by dissolving the glue. Use a rag dampened with ammonia or wax remover. Removing generations of grime reveals much about what's underneath. As well, the unstained inside of drawers and framework, when wet, can also give a useful show of the grain.

If soap and water don't do the trick, then use a pen-knife on an inconspicuous spot and scrape away either a small patch of paint or some layers of polish and varnish. The most straightforward way to decide whether to refinish is to find an unfinished piece or to strip a small section. Does this revealed wood look interesting? Does it suggest it's worth the time and effort to strip the whole piece down to bare wood, and then go through the process of re-staining and refinishing to bring out the hidden beauty in this piece of furniture?

Construction

What you have revealed may be any one of dozens of woods used in furniture making. There are two big "ifs" here: if the piece is veneered, then the finished top and unfinished bottom surfaces won't match — they won't even be close.

Veneers

Veneers are very thin: when working on them, be careful to use only fine grades of steel wool or sandpapers, never scrapers or edged tools, and protect the surface when you're working on the rest of the piece. If the wood is solid, and if you like the appearance, you can proceed with stripping all of it and treating it with a clear finish. If it's not exciting, perhaps restoring the finish is the best idea. Pine, poplar, birch or pecan is often given "oak," "walnut," "cherry" or "rosewood" finishes and sold as such.

Plywood

If the wood uncovered is plywood, then it will always be plywood. Edges can be covered or filled and a sturdy enamel paint applied, but that's about all that can be done. A lot of furniture is made of "lumber core plywood": it has a veneer on both sides, but only one side is used. Even more is made of particle board, sometimes with real, but very thin wood veneers, much more often of plastic printed with a wood grain pattern and applied to the board under high heat and pressure. If the only problem is that the furniture's present finish is absolutely unacceptable, then look for furniture enamels at a paint store, and think about how the new colour will fit in with the room. If a piece is plain, but useful, try using an enamel that matches the wall colour so the piece looks like it belongs in the room, but doesn't draw attention.

Dissection

There is another type of appraisal to be done on a large or elaborate piece, such as an old-fashioned dressing table, complete with mirror and maybe even candlestick stands. Can the parts of the piece stand alone? Perhaps the mirror could be a separate feature. Perhaps it's framed by an attractive wood, and made of deeply bevelled glass. It could easily be used as a wall mirror. The candlesticks can be removed and fashioned into wall lamp holders. What is left is a chest of drawers on legs, probably with two gaps in the top surface where the mirror was removed. You must decide whether it is within your ability to match this surface wood and produce a good top finish for this future distinctive piece of furniture, or you shouldn't start the job: you'll just wind up with three valueless pieces.

Armoire

Another example of an acquisition that's a candidate for imaginative dissection is one of those turn-of-the-century wardrobes or armoires, obviously built when bedrooms had three-metre high ceilings and were fairly large rooms. In all probability the mirrors set into the two doors are worth the cost of the piece plus whatever materials are needed for refurbishing. If they were removed, veneer panels could be inserted in the spaces previously occupied by the mirrors.

The whole piece offers a number of possibilities. Perhaps the top of the wardrobe can be quite easily separated from the bottom, which usually consists of two wide and deep drawers. If so, there's now the possibility of a free-standing cupboard suitably proportioned to a contemporary home, as well as a chest that can be ground-hugging or put on castors. The chest will require a new top, but the choice of materials is wide. The chest alone would be an ideal toy box for a youngster's bedroom, and the cupboard can serve as a fine extra closet.

Restoration

Restoration, in other words, does not have to be an "as-was" proposition. The scale of pieces of furniture designed in the days when space was not at a premium can, with imagination, lend themselves to the realization of two or three items for the price of one.

But if for whatever reason a piece of furniture becomes so attractive that you are ready to proceed, be assured of one thing — if you don't rush it, if you carefully read the labels of the materials you buy, and apply their contents equally carefully and don't try for a miraculous overnight renovation, you can obtain admirable results.

Remember too, that we can be more aware of fashion and style in furniture than we think we are. If you aren't happy with your furniture, ask yourself why. One of the things that "dates" a piece and makes it look old, or wrong, or fussy, may be the finish, the colour, or the hardware. If a set of drawers has missing or poor drawer pulls, simply replacing them before investing time and money in refinishing will tell you if more improvement could be worthwhile. Similarly, if a chair looks dark, heavy and lumpy but is comfortable and useful, think about a change in colour or upholstery to match what you see in modern furniture displays or show homes. As fashions in furniture change, most of that change will be superficial: chairs that are comfortable and sturdy will stay that way regardless of their colour, and you can change that easily by stripping and refinishing.

Stripping

Under **Preparation,** we mentioned tools, workplace and safety. If the essentials are available, then it's time to empty drawers, find another place for whatever is sitting on the table, or re-arrange the chairs while the selected one is being refinished.

If the furniture is solid, and doesn't require repairs of any kind, then consider whether to refinish it as one piece or reduce it to its major elements and do it piece by piece.

Typical pieces

Chairs

Chairs should not be disassembled if they don't need to be repaired, but if they have upholstery you don't want to damage, either cover the material with a good tight seal of plastic and tape, or remove it. Many frame chairs have seats that separate easily from the chair because the seat is the separate upholstered piece. If a chair is caned, or has a leather cushion, it must be protected.

Case Goods

Case goods — dressers, armoires, sets of shelves, desks, essentially any piece of furniture that is for all intents and purposes a box — should have its drawers removed and stripped to be refinished separately. Doors are a judgement call. If they're loose, sagging, out of square or warped, first remove and repair, then refit them before stripping and refinishing. If it will be awkward and time consuming to work on a piece with the doors on it, then obviously they should come off. In general, don't create extra work for yourself: if the screws and hinges are tight and well-fitting, the door square and true in the frame, leave it. Shelves should come out of any unit unless they're built into it, for example with dados. Consider removing the back, if it's a panel, to allow for easy working. Desks are often two-piece units and the top will be removable as one piece. Tambour (roll) tops are strips of wood with a cloth backing which ride in a groove in the desk side. They come out after the back panel of the desk is removed, or when the entire top is lifted. Paying attention to your own convenience and comfort will make a real difference to the quality of work you do when refinishing.

Mirrors and frames

A mirror is glass, and can break. Once it's gone, much of the value of the frame is too. If it's small and light enough to handle safely, mask the mirror and protect *both* surfaces. If the finish on the frame is so bad you must be able to work all around the wood, the mirror has to come out. Picture frames are similar but often removing the mattes and backing weakens a frame severely. If you're restoring a fine wood frame and don't care about what's inside it, leave it there to add strength during the handling it gets while you're working on it.

Tables: end tables, side tables

Most tables are two-piece units. The top is usually attached to the frame with glue, screws and metal clips or occasionally with bolts, or both. If screws alone have been used, you'll find them inside the apron (the frame on which the top of the table rests). If glue has been used, you'll find glue blocks inside the apron as well. If the top is secure, leave it on. If it's warped or loose, repair it first, refit it to make sure the job is right, and then refinish separately. The top is the most highly-finished part of the table: protect it from scratching or splashes by masking it off except when you're working on it. Many new dining tables have the apron permanently attached to the table top. The legs on these tables are removed by loosening the corner bolts.

Hardware: handles, door pulls, hinges, decorations

Keep every piece of hardware, with the screw or bolt that attached it, in a container. If you're stripping the hardware as well, let it sit in a closed jar with some stripper solution in the bottom. The fumes, and an occasional stir, will do most of the work for you.

What kind of finish does this thing have?

Identifying surface finishes is done through testing with solvents. Enamel paints are varnishes with color pigments, and are easy to identify. They need strippers to remove them; refinishers aren't strong enough. Make all these tests in a typical but not obvious spot on the furniture.

Shellac and lacquer are found on commercially made, not previously refinished wood furniture that has been stained or veneered. Use a wax remover first, before testing.

Shellac is tested by dropping or wiping denatured alcohol on its surface. The alcohol will soften the surface, which you can then spread with a cloth or finger. A bad shellac surface, one that's alligator-skinned or water marked with white streaks, can be restored (amalgamated) with denatured alcohol because of this softening.

Lacquer isn't affected by denatured alcohol, so test a surface that may be lacquer with alcohol first. Then use lacquer thinner. If the surface softens, it's lacquer, but a varnished surface will crack. A poor or slightly scratched or marked lacquer surface can also be amalgamated, using lacquer thinner applied carefully on a clean rag.

Varnish is affected by lacquer thinner and will crack and come off in patches. Paint removers or strippers will soften varnish so it can be scraped off. Test the quality of a varnish surface by rubbing it with the edge of a coin, the bottom of a spoon or a ring. If the tool leaves a white line in the surface, strip it.

Strippers

The label on the can of stripper will tell you how wonderful it is, how easy the job will be when you use it, what it's made of, and how much to use, usually expressed in an area measurement. You can ignore the first half of this information: the job is not going to be easy or fun, but the ingredients and the amount needed are essential information. Methylene chloride is the important ingredient in modern strippers, which are usually sold as liquids, or more expensively, as gels. If you're stripping a piece of case work, it's easy to estimate its area with the "length x width = area" rule, but a chair is a fussy thing to measure. Count on using a one-litre can for a dresser, half the can for a chair. When you buy your stripper, buy paint thinner and denatured alcohol for cleaning up the piece after stripping. Use a disposable nylon bristle or recycled brush for applying stripper — it will be good for no other use afterward.

Refinishers

Refinishers are a kind of stripper formulated to take off a surface finish like shellac, lacquer or varnish, but leave the underlying stain intact. A refinisher will cut down on your work if the stain and shade of your furniture piece is fine, but the surface finish is bad.

Scrapers

Scrapers should be smooth-bladed and have rounded corners. They don't need to be sharp — the chemical action of the stripper is doing the work and the blade is there to remove the resulting melted paint. Sharp-edged scrapers are for removing exterior paint. The smoothness of the blade is crucial, however — don't recycle old, rough tools for paint scrapers; the scratches and gouges they make in the surface will ruin it and your day. If you're using a heated scraper, one that uses hot air to soften and lift the paint, you may still find it handy to have some liquid stripper and hand scrapers for hard-to-reach corners and trim.

Stripping Basics

Start with the safety tips: long sleeve shirt, old but good pants, solid top shoes (no sandals), rubber kitchen gloves, (thin "surgical" gloves don't stand up to the work), eye protection, good ventilation, all sources of flame extinguished (including pilot lights and cigarettes), floor covered, and children and pets out of the way.

Don't pour the stripper onto the piece out of its own can: pour stripper into a container that you can comfortably hold, with a wide mouth. A tuna fish or coffee can are good examples. Use only part of the stripper, and seal the original container again. Dip your brush into the stripper and flow the stripper onto the horizontal surface of the furniture in front of you. Keep the area you cover small until you feel comfortable with the work. Start by covering three convenient areas with stripper. Putting down your stripper and brush, pick up another similar, empty can and your scraper. If the first area you covered is bubbled, wrinkled, or soft, start scraping. Keep the scraper at a very narrow angle to the work: your knuckles should almost be touching the surface. Work with the grain or direction of the wood. If the paint lifts easily, keep going. If not, wait. Paint will bubble or wrinkle, and varnish will blister or soften, as strippers work.

Disposal

You may have some problems disposing of paints and strippers and similar inflammable and toxic garbage, depending upon environmental regulations in your area. Usually, there will be special collection areas or days where you can take dangerous materials to designated locations.

> ## *Warning!*
>
> As the stripper breaks down the paint, fumes are given off, and the atmosphere can become dangerous if you don't have enough ventilation. *Any sign of headache, nausea or breathing difficulty is a warning to leave the area and get fresh air.* Use the empty can to hold paint and stripper you've removed — it is a dangerous solution, still capable of burning or staining anything it touches.

As you work from area to area, you may need to skip paint that won't lift, or reapply stripper if the action has slowed down too much. If you're working on a chair or table with turned legs, coarse steel wool held in your hand will wrap around the work and be faster to use. If steel wool is giving the wood a polished look, stop using it, and use an abrasive paper instead: the polished look is a spot where the pores of the wood have been closed up, and won't paint or stain properly later.

Keep moving your work so that the surface you're working on is horizontal, and at a comfortable height. When you're ready to stop, it's a good time to wash down the work with thinner or water and wipe the rest of the piece off. Protect the work, and seal all the cans, especially the one full of stripper and paint residue.

Stripping large smooth areas goes quickly unless the paint is very strong or in so many layers you have to reapply stripper continually. But every piece also has its corners and trim, areas where you'll need toothbrushes, skewers and toothpicks to move the softened paint away. If your furniture has been stripped and refinished previously, you may find it slow going. The only cure is patience — and more stripper.

If the paint is very glossy, or the varnish thick and new, use coarse sandpaper to open up the surface pores of the wood to allow the stripper to penetrate quickly.

It's a good general rule to do as much as you can, as quickly as you can, and come back to difficult spots later.

Painting Problems

The paint or finish won't all come off: try another product. If an ordinary stripper solution didn't complete the job, a gelled type that can sit on the area overnight may be the answer. If nothing will remove the finish, or it will not take paint, the surface may have been treated with milk paint, which may respond to ammonia, or with wax, silicone or a penetrating resin. Try using sealing solutions on the surface, shellac, and painting.

There's still residue in the corners or on the rungs or carving: use a smaller scraper or a rag on a pointed stick that can get into the depression. When the piece was made, the area may have been more deeply stained or filled, or the wood surface rougher, and it may not be possible to eliminate all traces of the finish.

The wood is an unpleasant color or a variety of shades: this may be the result of the chemicals in the stripper, but it's usually due to the original construction. Stripping does show how much finishing work will be necessary to bring back the original appearance. Consider using stains, which can be applied in successive coats, to even out the finish.

The surface is rough: stripping off the old finish has opened up the pores of the wood. Sanding is necessary now before applying the finishing coats. Start with a medium grade of abrasive, then use two finer grades.

After stripping

Once the job is done, let the furniture dry out for 24 hours. You may not want to look at it for a while anyway. Check to make sure it's still sturdy and there are no new cracks or faults to repair. Now is the time to revise any plans for finishing: if the wood you found is dull, a stain or paint is needed. If it's beautiful, a clear finish that shows it off is an obvious choice.

Personal Notes

Sanding, Painting and Staining

Sanding

Sanding does not have to be a chore or a bore. If you remember that it's possible to overdo sanding, and that only the final pass needs to be done by hand, you can take a constructive attitude to this essential step between stripping and refinishing.

Sanding basics

It is definitely possible to overdo sanding: don't sand with your hand alone. Use a sanding block or power sander. Don't round off corners or sand across or back along the wood grain. Don't use such a fine paper that it clogs, creating fine powder and filling the pores of the wood as well as your nose and lungs. Don't use a coarse paper and a lot of power and strength or you may scratch, groove or scar the surface.

Papers

Have a selection of papers from medium fine to very fine around. Sandpaper today is actually made of metallic particles, often on a cloth backing and better called "abrasives." It is sold in grades determined by the maker, but usually with descriptions like "coarse" or "fine" printed on the backing.

Carbide or oxide papers are your first choice, garnet next, flint last. If you're really stumped, buy a package with a selection of grades. Start sanding with the paper that doesn't clog up immediately. If the paper "clogs," it will pack solid with powder and just slide over the surface. As you work, feel the surface, and get your eye down to wood level, looking at it against the light — rough spots will be apparent.

Tools

The single best choice for a power sanding tool is an orbital sander. The worst is a disk sander on your electric drill — the rotating disk can't help but cut across the grain of the wood. "In line" sanders do very fine work, but are slower than orbitals, and belt sanders are far too likely to cut into the surface of the wood rather than smooth it. A vacuum attachment is a valuable accessory for any power sander. When buying abrasives for these machines, look for paper specified for use with power equipment.

Steel Wool

Steel wool in the finer grades — usually sold as 000 or 3/0 — is a good substitute for the finest grades of abrasive. Use it for the last smoothing before painting. Avoid creating a polished look on the wood surface.

Whether you use power tools, a sanding block or steel wool, remember to *always sand with the grain*. When you can see and feel that the surface is smooth, you're finished.

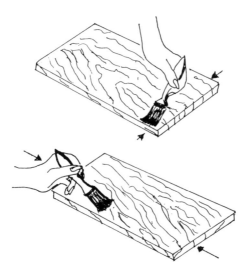

Use a vacuum cleaner and a tack rag before painting. This is a cloth damp with turpentine (see pg. 12), and its job is to get every last speck of powder off the surface and out of the pores of the wood.

Painting

If you have repaired, stripped and sanded a piece of furniture that was previously painted, it may have been with the idea of staining or varnishing it to display the wood grain. By now, you know whether the wood is attractive enough, or if you should repaint. Some furniture, for children's rooms for example, really needs to be painted to be useful.

Painting basics

The paint for furniture is enamel, usually in a high gloss finish. Generally, alkyd and polyurethane-based enamels are more washable and durable than latex or acrylics. Paint mixing today is capable of giving you whatever colour you want; if your dresser has to match the drapes, take a drape with you to the paint store.

Coverage

Coverage is the area one coat of paint will cover; most furniture should have a minimum of two coats and three is much better. If the paint label recommends an undercoat or primer, use it. Otherwise, thin the first coat before applying it for good penetration of the wood.

Work with the paint as you did with the stripper — keep the surface horizontal and at a convenient height. Painting should be done in a warm, dust-free area with good light.

Drying

Try to work where you can leave your furniture to dry undisturbed for at least the time required by the label. Most enamels must dry and have a light sanding with very fine sandpaper between coats: but polyurethane-based paints must usually have the second coat before the first is dry.

Work with as large a brush as you can hold: it is much faster, the paint is applied more smoothly, with fewer ridges, overlaps, air bubbles and missed spots.

It is usually more convenient to paint the trim after the whole piece is done in the base colour. Use masking tape made for painting, and only apply it after the base coat is thoroughly dry, to avoid marking the paint. Press the edges of the tape down well to avoid paint running under the tape.

Paint drawers and shelves separately. Finishing the insides of drawers and the backs of shelves is an important quality touch, and helps prevent warping of the wood.

Humidity has a slowing effect on paint drying. Allow more time in rainy weather.

Painting problems

Bubbles: stir, don't shake paint used on furniture. Shaking fills the paint with air.

Brush marks and streaks on the surface: they are caused by "brushing out" the paint too far. Flow the paint onto the surface so that it can level out on its own. It's simply a matter of practise and experience to get it right.

The paint won't stick in some places: usually, there's stripper or other chemicals still in the wood. Seal knots with shellac if they're present in never-painted wood. The only cure for areas that won't take paint is stripping down again. If there's wax in the wood, it must be sanded out; paint will never stick over wax.

Runs and streaks in the paint: too much paint, especially on a vertical surface. Keep a rag handy while painting and catch runs. If they show up on a dry surface, sand them down.

The paint won't dry: drying time varies greatly, especially due to humidity. If you're sanding between coats, you must allow much more time for drying — up to eight times as long.

Staining

There are many difficult and elaborate ways to stain furniture. The easiest method is to use gelled stains which are applied by wiping them onto the furniture surface with a rag, and wiping off when you like the shade. In all respects they are the simplest and best way to stain.

Staining basics

Stains are sold by the name of the wood they are mixed to imitate, not the wood you will use them on. Our image of "walnut" for example is of a dark, heavy wood, because so many light woods are stained dark to look like "walnut." It's better to pick your stain from a colour chart than from preconceived notions, to match the room or the use you have for the piece.

Stains aren't particular; they'll stain anything. So wear rubber gloves, old clothes and work on a protected floor, or you will have walnut hands, shirt and carpet as well as furniture.

Application

Stains, unlike paints, can be applied more heavily in some places on the furniture, and should be applied more lightly in others. If the seat of a platform chair has a light board in it, several applications of stain on that board can smooth out the appearance. Edge or end grain, always found on the edges of curved table tops that haven't been lipped or edge-veneered will soak up stain and turn darker than the rest of the piece because that grain is so much more open than on the flat surfaces. Use more sealer or filler on end grain, and when sanding, always finish end grain with the finest paper you have. This seals the ends because the fine abrasive does not tear the pores. Then, either use less stain on the end grain, or wipe it off more quickly. Ideally, you want your piece to have the same shade throughout; practically, you want it to be close.

Staining should be done quickly: keep the rags moving, applying the stain and wiping it off. Do each part of the piece in turn, with the most visible – the top – done last. As a rule, don't do only part of a surface. Do all of it, or the stain applied later won't match.

Test patch

When staining, don't let the simplicity and ease of applying a gelled stain lead you astray: it is easy to overstain, making the piece too dark, with the grain barely visible and the beauty of the wood gone. If you can, stain an inconspicuous spot on the wood – the bottom of the chair frame rails, the side of the dresser that will face the corner of the room, the inside of a table leg or part of the apron – and wait to see how you like the result. If it's fine, you've only lost some time; if it's not, you've saved having to strip the piece again.

Filling

Filling follows staining if you're staining an open-grained wood. Oak or mahogany, for example, have large, open pores. Wood fillers made for furniture refinishing are used after staining. They fill the pores and accent the oak grain. Once the filler is applied and then mostly wiped off, leaving only the particles in the pores on the piece, the furniture must be sealed, preferably with a varnish, shellac or lacquer.

Staining problems

Light streaks: apply more stain on these areas.

Part of the wood is darker than other parts: when staining, apply the stain to the entire piece quickly, and don't overlap dried stain with new. When doing a chair, wipe the stain on an entire leg or rung, not half of it. With large areas like table tops, do them last so they aren't marked when handling the rest of the piece, keeping the coat thin, and rub it out — extending it as much as you can. Don't let it "puddle" or sit without being wiped.

Clear finishes

If your furniture is made of a high quality, fine furniture wood — maple, oak, walnut or teak — it can easily take a clear finish that protects it from body oils, food stains and spills while allowing the natural wood colour to show through and be appreciated. "Natural" comes and goes in popularity. At one time, even very fine woods were automatically painted or stained. Finishing techniques are similar to staining or painting depending upon the product you choose. Urethane-based clear finishes are clear and strong, and quite easy to apply. "Plastic" or "vinyl" finishes are stronger, but tend to be permanent: the wood can't be refinished later.

Pick clear finishes on the basis of where the furniture is going to be used: strong, moisture-resistant finishes like plastics in kitchens, dining rooms, and softer, warmer toned stains for living areas. If quick results are necessary — you have only a weekend for furniture refinishing — look for quick-drying finishes.

Personal Notes

Finishing

The grain and texture of the wood in your furniture is emphasized, even exaggerated, by the stain you apply. But the beauty of the furniture comes from the finishing coats that give an illusion of depth and life to the surface.

As with staining, there are difficult and elaborate ways to create this effect, but the simple and straightforward way to get the result you want is to use a polyurethane varnish, sand between coats with superfine or 400 abrasive, and coat the piece a minimum of three times. The maximum is up to you — some grand pianos have had thirty coats of varnish to get that deep, lustrous look.

Using a modern varnish is simple, but like many simple things, it has to be done right.

Varnishing basics

Start by ensuring that the room in which you work is warm, dry and spotless. Vacuum everything and go over the piece with a tack rag to get every speck of dust off of it. Leave the room for a few hours and let the dust you've raised settle:

then come in and clean again. It will be worth it, because nothing attracts and shows dust specks like a new varnish finish.

Use a new, high-quality natural bristle brush — about 75 mm is a good size for furniture — and use it only for varnishing. Don't let it dry between coats. Keep it immersed in a varnish thinner or mineral spirits.

Avoiding air bubbles

Unless the varnish maker gives contrary instructions, never shake, stir or mix the varnish. Let it sit still for an hour before using it, and don't rub the brush against the lip of the can when removing it. All of this helps prevent air bubbles. Every air bubble in your varnish will become a crater on the surface of your furniture.

Application

Apply varnish by flowing it onto a horizontal surface from the brush, lifting the brush at the end of each stroke, not overlapping but just joining new strokes, and try to work smoothly. Have a good light source shining across the surface you're painting, to reveal dust or spots you've missed.

Because varnishes reveal mistakes so well, avoid problems by working carefully. Where it is necessary to work on vertical surfaces — chair legs for example — keep coats thinner, and cover smaller areas so you can catch and control runs and drips.

On large flat areas — shelves or desk tops — it's recommended that you apply each coat of varnish in a pattern. Brushing across the grain, cover a comfortable sized area; no more than a foot square to start. Then, brushing with the

grain, and with the brush held almost straight up and down and the ends of the bristles just touching the new, wet surface, go over it again. This system of brushing on varnish and then going back over it at right angles ensures that your coat will be smooth and no spots will be missed. Avoid overworking your varnish job; once across with the grain, once across against the grain and then move on to the next square. Always complete the job at one time, and never leave part of the surface unvarnished.

Drying

Leave the furniture alone when you've finished and keep the room closed up for at least the drying time specified on the can. Test for dryness with a fingernail − if you can see the mark, let it dry longer.

Always sand between coats, but wait at least twice the drying time before starting to sand, and very carefully remove dust before the next coat is applied. Remember that the reason for sanding is only to provide a surface for the next coat to adhere to, and to take off any dust or specks.

Varnishing problems

The varnish coat is too shiny: the coat needs rubbing. Use felt or a similar soft, clean rag, and "cut polish" sold for use on car finishes. Test your rubbing first, on a small, inconspicuous area, not on the middle of the table top.

The varnish coat isn't shiny enough: polish it with very fine steel wool: use grades like 4/0, 0000 or finer.

Polishing doesn't give it the gloss or depth you want: use more coats of varnish, sanding between each. If you've used a semi-gloss rather than a glossy varnish, you may have to switch. It's easier to tone down a glossy coat than to brighten a semi-gloss.

Other finishes

Shellac and lacquer are traditional furniture finishes. Both are used on commercially made pieces because they are fast drying and can be sprayed on. If you decide to employ them, use the same techniques as for varnishing. Follow the maker's instructions very carefully — both are far harder to use with good results than varnishes.

Rubbing oil, not penetrating oil finish, is an old finishing technique that produces a fine result on good hardwoods, but needs constant care, including yearly refinishing, and attracts dust like no other surface.

Waxing or Polishing

Wax creates a renewable, expendable surface that will help you avoid going through what you've just done — refinishing a piece of furniture because the surface was damaged. It will also make it look great, and attract admiration.

Waxing or polishing is necessary for furniture which has a lacquer or shellac finish to keep water, alcohol and other common household fluids away from those easily damaged surfaces.

Wax

Waxes are based on plant products like carnauba, while polishes are based on mineral oils and solvents. The short answer if you're trying to decide between them is: wax.

Waxing is also necessary for any furniture which has a natural, clear finish. Many good finishes — like "Danish oil" — don't shine. An oil or stain will have added some life to the surface, but it needs the wax to create the gloss. The wax coating also absorbs the impacts of daily life that might otherwise go right into the wood.

Wax alone has been used from the dawn of furniture making to finish bare wood. *Don't* use it as a bare wood finish if you will ever want to do any other kind of finishing: once wax is in the wood pores, it will not come out, allow any finish to take over it, or take paint.

Carnauba

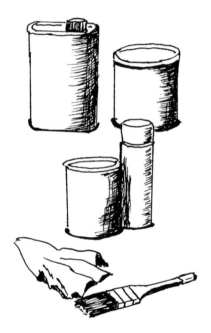

The single best and most expensive wax is carnauba, and a good quality paste wax will be half carnauba.

Polishes sold on the basis of their ease of use will be mainly oils and solvents, with small amounts of wax. They're mainly cleaners and brighteners, where as paste wax will apply a coating of some depth to the surface.

The problem is that paste wax has to be applied by hand, and rubbed and rubbed to produce the polished look you want. A buffer on an electric drill is a great paste waxing accessory, but the hand work to apply it is unavoidable.

Polish

Similarly, don't use a polish containing silicone on any piece of wood furniture that you value, and may want to refinish in the future. The silicone enters the wood fibers and prevents any finish from holding, even after complete stripping and sanding.

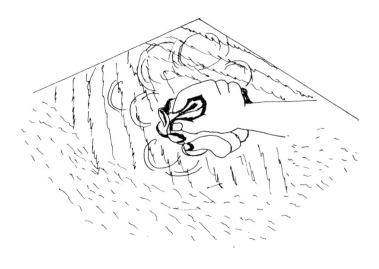

Waxing basics

Waxing with paste wax is not a complicated chore. Dust the surface that will be waxed first, and don't use that cloth for waxing, or you may scratch the surface you're trying to protect. Waxing requires a clean, soft cloth large enough to fill your fist so you have a good grip on it. Rub the cloth into the paste wax can, and then on the surface, and keep at it, checking the surface against the light. Many waxes will have a cloudy appearance that dissappears with drying, at which time you begin buffing the surface. Count on using three coats of wax for a good job, but one or two are certainly far better than none.

Wax, once applied, becomes a part of housework. The wear any furniture gets means that the wax coating is removed, and must be replaced. This eventually results in a lot of wax on untouched areas, and therefore the need to use a wax remover, and to wax again.

Waxing problems

The wax doesn't seem to work, it was shiny when I put it on, but the shine disappeared: you need a better quality wax, and more coats of it.

How do I know when the wax is buffed hard enough: hard wax coats won't show fingerprints.

French Polishing

A word about French Polishing; this is a technique of applying shellac mixed with turpentine on a pad held in the hand. The pad is kept constantly moving over the surface, and the heat and friction of the pad applies a thin coating of the shellac to the surface. There is no limit to the number of coats that can be used, but the *minimum* is seven to ten. Anything that comes in a can and promises to give you a "French polish" finish with no work is, at best, a polish with a lot of solvent and silicone, and a waste of money.

Terms and Words

Antiquing

At its most sophisticated, antiquing goes to great lengths to create a look of the wear and tear of centuries and even of ancient stains and worm-holes. An antique look can be simply achieved by buying a "kit" which usually consists of a glaze that is applied and then partially wiped off at certain points to simulate a mellowed and aged look.

Bleach

Used to remove inherent stains and sometimes to give wood a fashionable "blond" look. Bleaches are applied after the old finish has been stripped off. There are commercial brands stocked at paint stores. Household bleaches containing sodium hypochlorite work just as well. Oxalic acid, diluted as directed, or 30 percent hydrogen peroxide can also be used. To neutralize bleaching action, use either undiluted vinegar or borax mixed at the rate of 250 mL (1 cup) to one litre of water.

Brushes

Use a new brush even for stripping off old finishes. You are working with caustic materials, and however clean a paintbrush appears to be, some left-over paint is invariably going to work its way down from the handle. After use, keep it separate, soaking in a can of mineral spirits, with some cover to prevent evaporation.

Crayons

These are coloured wax sticks sold by most well-stocked hardware or paint stores and used, when melted, to patch particularly deep scratches, cigarette burns or chip marks.

Crazing

Think of cracked, parched earth and you've got the idea — an array of fine lines on the wood's surface, usually the result of long-term exposure to sunlight. The solution is to replace the oils and recover accordingly.

Denatured alcohol

This is a type of alcohol used as a thinner, particularly for shellac. It has been "denatured" by the addition of chemicals that are intended to make it utterly undrinkable.

Distressing

This word is part of the jargon used by the modern antique manufacturer, and it describes those actions that are taken to make a piece of furniture look both old and well used. Distressing produces the dents, scratches, stains and burns of alleged antiquity. Chains are sometimes used to hit the piece, scarring the surface. In some cases, woodworm holes are literally drilled into the wood. Some carpenters even set the piece outside so that the weathering effects of the sun and rain can work on it for weeks on end.

Fillers

These can be crayons or pastes used for repair jobs. But for a fine-quality finish on wood that has been completely stripped, an appropriate filler paste should be rubbed into the surface after it has been properly sealed. Some woods require no filler. Those with a noticeable grain structure (woods such as oak, chestnut or ash) benefit by rubbing filler paste (made of finely crushed, inert rock) across the grain. When smooth, give the piece another sealer coat.

Finishers

After you have spent so much time and care revealing the character of the piece of furniture and staining it, it needs protection. Today, manufacturers offer a range of poly-urethane varnishes that will give woodwork a high gloss, a low or satin gloss, or a no-gloss finish. Oil and shellac-based finishes reveal the beauties of particularly interesting woods, but neither of them have the toughness needed for a much-used piece of furniture; both require polishing or waxing afterwards.

Inlay, Marquetry and Veneer

Inlay, marquetry, veneer — in all cases this means thin pieces of decorative or scarce woods applied to a different wood core piece — for example, a strip of sandalwood or tulipwood inlaid on oak. A favourite motif for such pieces built in the late 18th century was a scrolled sea shell. Complex designs and mosaics can include such woods as walnut, holly, ebony and rose, all being wafer-thin shavings from a piece of stock. Many hardware and lumber stores carry an assortment of veneer material, either for the ambitious furniture builder or re-finisher, or just for simple repairs.

Lacquers

Lacquers were the old way to finish furniture. Now, thanks to the pressurized can as much as anything, they are the modern and relatively quick way to achieve an unblemished surface. This seemingly ever-expanding line of products has certainly replaced shellac in the popularity polls (which had earlier replaced lacquer). To repair or test for a lacquer finish, one must use a lacquer thinner. Shellac, which is more traditional, can only be dispatched with a paint remover.

Oil

A really fine example of antique furniture is most likely to have been finished with an oil-based polish. Lots of love and patience can replicate what is considered the highest compliment to a beautiful piece of carpentry. The basic ingredient of oil polishes is boiled linseed oil mixed with pure turpentine in the ratio of three to one. Add a few drops of japan (a drier), and warm the mixture up very carefully in a double-boiler (to avoid splashes and fires). This is applied to your furniture, the excess wiped off and then polished vigorously. The process is repeated again one to two weeks after the first application and thence up to twenty more times for a memorable, hard-as-glass finish. Today, there are modern oil concoctions that are easier to apply, dry more quickly and, to the untrained eye, still give that special look to a favourite piece.

Paints

Any paint is essentially a suspension of a pigment in a liquid. These days the paint industry offers a complexity of choices — paint that is oil-based, water-based, alkyd resin-based, based on acrylic esters and other polymers, latex paint or even a milk-based paint. Modern paints have their complimentary lines of strippers.

Very occasionally, the craftsman will uncover furniture that has been treated with milk paint. This was made with milk casein or milk powder and it was a common "wash" paint for barns a hundred years ago. Milk paints really invade wood and about the only thing that will remove them is ammonia. On the other hand, the smoky white finish of wood, particularly of solid oak or oak-finished furniture, is back in fashion, so one may only have to sand down and then finish up the surface. If the exposed wood isn't very interesting and you decide to repaint, prepare the surface as professionally as possible and, before painting, make sure it's completely dust-free.

Use high-quality brushes, and paint evenly with the grain. Enamel paints are especially popular because they eliminate the need for later glossing, but with enamels it is most important not to overload the brush. Also, carefully brush on the paint with a slight overlap which should then be smoothed over with more delicate brushwork; this will leave the surface virtually free of lines.

Patina

This is a word that exists almost only in the eye of the beholder. It relates to the look or the feel of a piece of furniture that has been dusted and polished for years, and which shows its wear and tear with grace. It is the subtle evidence of age, the gleam of a well-loved and well-cared-for article.

Pumice

Most furniture finishers have no use for sandpaper, partly because of the hardness of its abrasive abilities, partly because its edge, even using a sanding block, can quickly cause a streak or outright cut in a surface. As explained earlier, steel wool is recommended for surface sanding and for the polishing process. But for that final finish, pumice (which is lava rock) can be bought in powder form and made into a paste with lemon or mineral oil to control the degree of gloss.

Rottenstone

If pumice is the start of the final finish of a project, then rottenstone is the end of this final stage — an even softer abrasive that brings about a gloss that is deeply luxurious without glaring.

Sealers

If you've arrived at bare wood with an interesting grain and you want to proceed no further in the furniture's restoration, the marketplace now has the product you're looking for — the "Danish Oil" sealer. This penetrates the surface, stains the wood according to your preference and provides you with a surface that can be wax-polished. Modern sealing oils are manufactured from a synthetic resin but they can only be applied to raw wood because the finish is actually in the wood itself. Finally, sealers can be buffed with fine steel wool, or they can be glossed, depending on the final look and finish desired.

Shellac

The source for shellac is the lac bug, which is a native of India. It is made into a varnish by being dissolved in denatured alcohol and can be bought as a clear finish or one that is almost amber-hued. Shellac dries evenly and quickly and buffs up beautifully. But it has its disadvantages: alcohol dissolves it, and damp cups or pop cans leave white rings on the surface. So shellac requires a really well-matured wax protection, which is one reason why this old favourite of furniture makers has now often been replaced by less vulnerable finishes.

Stains

Stains come in many forms and serve many purposes. Pigmented stains are generally oil-based. Because the pigment is invariably in suspension, frequent stirring is vital. On the other hand, penetrating oil stains do just that — they penetrate the grain, without any highlights of colour. Finally and perhaps best of all the stains are the water stains, or even denatured alcohol stains, in which aniline-type dyes are completely dissolved. Because they're fast-acting, deeply penetrating and have a habit of raising the wood grain, one needs to be somewhat skilled to choose them.

Such stains are best applied by sponge; overlapping must be avoided because of the speed of their effectiveness. Otherwise, the beginning refinisher should have no problems. Generally, stains can enhance an interesting grain, or they can change an uninteresting grain into pleasing-looking wood. If you are staining, but not just to re-set a wood's natural colour, find an inconspicuous spot on which to experiment. Stains that seem light enough on the product label, or on a sample board in the hardware or stain store, often produce a darker-than-anticipated result at home. If possible, take a piece of wood of the desired colour to the store and ask to try the chosen stain first. One can always darken a stain, but to lighten it again is a massive chore.

Steel Wool

Because sandpapers clog, scratch and tear, any sanding that requires a fine finish should be done with steel wool. Steel wool is usually sold like skeins of wool, a number of rolls in one box or bag. There are usually seven grades available in a good hardware or paint store. Of the seven — 3, 2, 1, 0 (fine), 00 (sometimes called 2/0 or very fine), 000 (3/0 or extra fine) and 0000 (4/0 or super fine) — only those between 0 and 0000 should be used on woodwork. Steel wool has the advantage of being used in a ball so that it leaves no edge. It can clean away corners and fine moldings without leaving any scratch or finish marks. Unlike sandpaper, it can be rinsed in hot water and re-cycled. But don't leave wet steel wool lying around: it rusts very quickly. The finish to any polish, manufactured or wax-based, that can be given to a fine piece of furniture by a final series of deft movements with super-fine steel wool is something that will bring joy to the beginner's eyes.

Stripping

If your first task is to remove layers of lurid paint, the marketplace is ready to help with a wide variety of products — but all deliver essentially similar results. One should always strip paint while it is still gooey from the application of stripper. If a section has dried out it suggests that the chemical activity in the stripper has not penetrated far enough, so apply more stripper, to cause more bubbling to take place.

Apart from commercial strippers, there are do-it-yourself chemicals such as lye and trisodium phosphate. These will do an excellent job at little cost, but you must stop the action with pure vinegar, because both these chemicals have a tendency to darken the wood. They also cause a raising of the wood grain which will almost certainly require additional sanding after their use. As well, good paint and hardware stores sell appropriate varnish removers. Their chemical alternative is ammonia or lye. In either case, one should work outdoors because of the fumes, and there should be plenty of water available because ammonia and lye can burn skin. Left too long on a wooden surface, they will cause darkening.

Tack rags

These are a minor essential, if there can be such a thing, to any serious undertaking involving the stripping and refinishing of furniture. Sawdust and air-borne dust are the bane of a fine enamel or finishing job. The most obvious dust can be vacuumed off, but there will still remain an almost invisible enemy that sooner or later will accumulate on the brush and remain as exasperating and impossible-to-remove blemishes in the midst of all that patient handiwork. Enter the tack rag. All that's required is a pad (multi-layered) of cheesecloth that's been dampened with water. A few drops of turpentine and an equal amount of varnish are added. Now squeeze this tack rag as if it were bread dough, then turn it back into a pad; when used, it will remove all dust particles without leaving a clue as to its magic ingredients.

Thinners

These are solvents which simply extend the pigmentation of a paint or stain. When buying an oil-based paint, it's a good idea to buy a thinner that is either turpentine or turpentine-based at the same time. If the chosen colour is satisfactory, the thinner can still be used to clean and store your paint brush. Alkyd paints require mineral spirit thinners. Latex and milk-based paints can be diluted with water. The recommended thinner is always listed on the label of lacquers, enamels and shellacs. Be sure to buy the correct one.

Tourniquet

Frequently when repairing and refinishing old furniture, one will come across a spindle that rattles in its base, a drawer joint that is loose, or banding that has begun to flap. If water has been used to any extent during the refinishing process, the glue used to hold the piece together will inevitably absorb some of the resulting moisture which will eventually cause joints to loosen. This is when re-glueing becomes necessary.

When appropriate clamps aren't available or when the areas involved are irregular in shape, the best way to obtain a new, tight fit is to wrap a strong piece of material (clothesline or rope) several times around the object, insert a hefty stick between some of the strands, twist until there is a very secure fit, and then tie the end of the stick in place until the glue is dry. If some shrinkage has occurred in the joint over the course of time, insert either wood slivers or tooth picks into the gap after applying the glue. Once the glue has dried, the protruding slivers of wood can easily be sawn off and smoothed down.

Wax

Waxes tend to be marketed as though they are elixirs, with magical properties. The truth is that most are based on either beeswax, paraffin wax, candelilla or carnauba. Each, or some of each in combination, are generally mixed with pure paraffin or pure turpentine to form either a paste or a liquid polish. Beeswax produces a somewhat dull finish. Candelilla, a derivative of a plant grown in Mexico, gives a much harder and more brilliant finish. The hardest finish of all comes from the repeated application and buffing of carnauba, which comes from a tree found growing chiefly in Brazil.